BRAZIL
the culture

Malika Hollander

A Bobbie Kalman Book

The Lands, Peoples, and Cultures Series

Crabtree Publishing Company
www.crabtreebooks.com

The Lands, Peoples, and Cultures Series

Created by Bobbie Kalman

Coordinating editor
Ellen Rodger

Production coordinator
Rosie Gowsell

Project development, photo research, design, and editing
First Folio Resource Group, Inc.
  Erinn Banting
  Tom Dart
  Claire Milne
  Jaimie Nathan
  Debbie Smith

Prepress and printing
Worzalla Publishing Company

Consultants
Lêda Leitão Martins, Cornell University; John M. Norvell, Cornell University

Photographs
AFP/Corbis/Magma: p. 11; Mary Altier: p. 5 (top); George Ancona/ImageState: p. 18 (left); AP/Wide World Photos: p. 9, p. 13, p. 17 (right), p. 21 (top), p. 22; Nair Benedicto, D. Donne Bryant Stock: p. 15, p. 17 (left), p. 28 (left); Barnabas Bosshart/Corbis/Magma: p. 8 (left); Jan Butchofsky-Houser/Corbis/Magma: p. 12 (left); Marc Crabtree: cover, title page, p. 4 (bottom), p. 5 (both), p. 6, p. 12 (right), p. 19 (left), p. 21 (bottom), p. 25 (bottom), p. 26 (both), p. 27 (right), p. 28 (right); Craig Duncan, D. Donne Bryant Stock: p. 5 (bottom); Robert Fried: p. 7 (bottom), p. 19 (right); Arvind Garg/Corbis/Magma: p. 10; Hulton-Deutsch Collection/Corbis/Magma: p. 20; Randall Hyman: p. 23 (right); Stephanie Maze/Corbis/Magma: p. 7 (top), p. 8 (right), p. 16, p. 23 (left); Suzanne Murphy-Larronde, D. Donne Bryant Stock: p. 4 (top); Museu Nacional Belas Artes, Rio de Janeiro, Brazil/Bridgeman Art Library/*Coffee Plantation* by Candido Portinari: p. 25 (top); Diego Lezama Orezzoli/Corbis/Magma: p. 27 (left); Fridman Paulo/Corbis/Magma: p. 29; Reuters NewMedia Inc./Corbis/Magma: p. 14 (left); Ricardo Teles, D. Donne Bryant Stock: p. 14 (right); Julia Waterlow/Eye Ubiquitous/Corbis/Magma: p. 24; Stan Wayman/Photo Researchers: p. 18 (right)

Illustrations
Dianne Eastman: icon
Ben Hodson: pp. 30–31
David Wysotski, Allure Illustrations: back cover

Cover: A woman from Salvador wears a colorful skirt and headdress traditionally worn by *Baianas*, or the women of Bahia, a state in Brazil.

Title page: Mass band members in colorful costumes prepare to entertain the crowds at the *Carnaval* festival, in the southeastern city of Rio de Janeiro

Icon: The *cavaquinho*, which appears at the head of each section, is a stringed musical instrument originally from Portugal. Traditional Brazilian music styles, such as the *samba*, use *cavaquinhos* as part of their distinctive sound.

Back cover: The toco toucan lives in Brazil's rainforests. It uses its large bill to snap up fruit on branches that are hard to reach.

All ready to go! Photographer Marc Crabtree spent several weeks photographing Brazil for this book.

Published by
Crabtree Publishing Company

PMB 16A,	612 Welland Avenue	73 Lime Walk
350 Fifth Avenue	St. Catharines	Headington
Suite 3308	Ontario, Canada	Oxford OX3 7AD
New York	L2M 5V6	United Kingdom
N.Y. 10118		

Cataloging-in-Publication Data
Hollander, Malika.
   Brazil. The culture / Malika Hollander.
     p. cm. -- (Lands, peoples, and cultures)
Includes index.
Summary: Text and photos show how the people of Brazil celebrate holidays and festivals, using art, music, dance, and stories.
   ISBN 0-7787-9340-0 (RLB) -- ISBN 0-7787-9708-2 (PB)
   1. Brazil--Civilization--Juvenile literature. 2. Brazil--Social life and customs--Juvenile literature. [1. Brazil--Civilization. 2. Brazil--Social life and customs.] I. Title: Culture. II. Title. III. Series: Lands, peoples, and cultures.
F2510.H659 2003
981--dc21

2003001266
LC

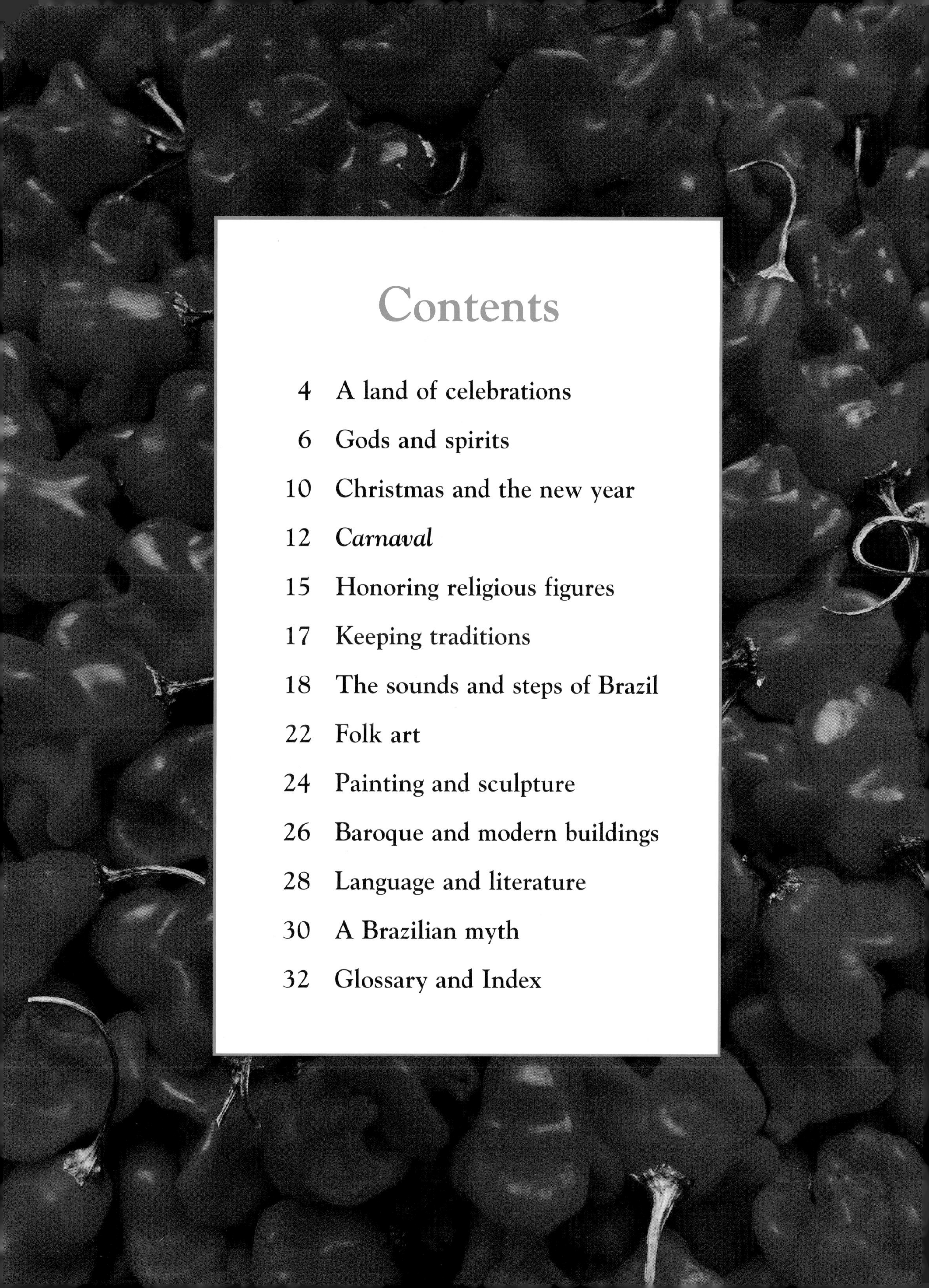

Contents

4   A land of celebrations

6   Gods and spirits

10   Christmas and the new year

12   *Carnaval*

15   Honoring religious figures

17   Keeping traditions

18   The sounds and steps of Brazil

22   Folk art

24   Painting and sculpture

26   Baroque and modern buildings

28   Language and literature

30   A Brazilian myth

32   Glossary and Index

🎸 A land of celebrations 🎸

Brazilians tell a story about an African slave named Pai Francisco who took care of his owner's favorite bull. One day, while the owner was away, Pai Francisco's pregnant wife pleaded with her husband to kill the bull so she could satisfy her craving for beef tongue. When the owner returned, he was furious to discover that his bull was dead. He threatened to kill Pai Francisco, but a healer used his special powers to bring the bull back to life. Pai Francisco was saved.

The tale of Pai Francisco and the bull is acted out during the festival of *Bumba-meu-boi*, which has many other names, including *Boi-Bumba* and *Bois-de-Reis*. Music and dancing fill the streets as people dressed as bulls pretend to attack onlookers. Brazil's **indigenous**, Portuguese, and African peoples all celebrate this festival, but each group has its own traditions, types of instruments, and styles of dance that give the holiday a different flavor wherever it is celebrated.

Musicians practice beating out a rhythm on their drums before the Carnaval *in Rio de Janeiro.*

(top) People dressed in bull costumes act out the story of Bumba-meu-boi, *in which a bull is brought back to life. In June, the northeastern city of São Luís holds Brazil's largest Bumba-meu-boi festival.*

The northeastern city of Salvador was once the capital of Brazil. Government offices, churches, mansions, and other historic buildings have been carefully preserved.

A blend of cultures

Festivals are not the only part of Brazilian life that combines cultures. Brazil's official language is a version of Portuguese that includes thousands of words from African and indigenous languages. Roman Catholicism is the country's main religion, but African and indigenous beliefs are often mixed in. Brazilian music also combines instruments, singing styles, and rhythms brought by different peoples.

Groups in the southeastern city of Rio de Janeiro compete against one another to create the best costumes for Carnaval.

Intricate gold carvings cover the walls and altar of a Catholic Church in Salvador.

Brazil's indigenous people came to the country about 11,000 years ago. They crossed a land bridge from Asia to North America, then traveled south to the lush rainforests and grassy plains of Brazil. There, they lived in harmony with nature. According to indigenous people's traditional beliefs, all living things and all elements of nature have a spirit. Religious leaders, called shamans, communicate with these spirits. They ask good spirits for help and guidance, and drive evil spirits away.

Roman Catholicism

Portuguese explorers and settlers arrived in Brazil in the early 1500s. They brought their religion, Roman Catholicism, with them. Roman Catholicism is a **denomination** of Christianity. Like other Christians, Roman Catholics believe in God, and they follow the teachings of his son on earth, Jesus Christ. Roman Catholics also believe in holy people called saints, through whom God performs miracles. They pray to saints for help in times of need and thank them for their blessings.

Missionaries

Catholic **missionaries** called Jesuits first arrived from Portugal in 1549. They came to give Portuguese settlers religious guidance and to **convert** indigenous people to Christianity. Jesuits gathered indigenous people into villages called *aldeias*. Indigenous people in *aldeias* were protected from slavery, unlike other indigenous people, but they could not practice their traditional ways of life or follow their beliefs. As well, many died from European diseases to which they had no **resistance**.

Miracle workers

Northeastern Brazil has been home to many miracle workers and **preachers** who claim that the current world is ending and that a better world is about to begin. Father Cícero Romão Batista became famous in 1889 after "the miracle of the host." One Sunday, he was giving communion, a ceremony during which Catholics eat a host, or wafer, and drink wine. The wafer represents the body of Christ, and the wine represents Christ's blood.

When blood appeared on a worshiper's host, people were convinced that it was Jesus' blood and that Father Cícero had performed a miracle. They began to save everything that Father Cícero touched — even clipped fingernails. People still honor Father Cícero, who died in 1934, by making **pilgrimages** to his grave in the northeastern town of Juazeiro do Norte and by placing images of him around their homes.

Each year, people go on a pilgrimage to Juazeiro do Norte to visit the grave of Father Cícero, the priest who founded the town in the 1920s.

Christianity today

Today, almost 75 percent of Brazil's population is Catholic, and religion plays an important part in people's lives. Catholic organizations build hospitals, orphanages, and churches, and feed and provide shelter for the poor. Priests help people who are homeless find homes, and help people who are landless find land. People of other Christian denominations also live in Brazil, including Presbyterians, Methodists, Episcopalians, Anglicans, Lutherans, Pentecostals, Baptists, and Mormons.

Catholics pray and leave offerings at this outdoor shrine, which is decorated with a cross and religious figurines.

A man wearing decorative body paint participates in a Candomblé ceremony in the northern city of Belém.

African gods and goddesses

Some of Brazil's Roman Catholics combine their religious beliefs with the beliefs of the country's indigenous people and people of African **descent**. African slaves were brought to Brazil beginning in the 1600s to work on **plantations**, in mines, and in cities. The main African-Brazilian religion is Candomblé, which means "to dance in honor of the gods." It is practiced mostly in Salvador, in the northeast. People who follow Candomblé believe in one supreme being, Olorum or Olodumaré, and many gods and goddesses, called *orixás*. *Orixás* control the forces of nature and protect people on earth. Oxalá, the god of **fertility** and the harvest, and Iemanjá, the goddess of the sea, are two of the most important *orixás*.

Dances for the gods

Followers of Candomblé perform ceremonies in which they communicate with *orixás*. The ceremonies are usually held in a spirit house, called a *terreiro*, and are led by a *pai de santo*, or father of the saint, or *mãe de santo*, or mother of the saint. The main part of the ceremony is the offering of a meal to the *orixás*. The offering usually includes an animal that has been **sacrificed**. Then, *filhos* or *filhas de santo*, or sons or daughters of the saint, chant and dance to the beating of drums. The *orixás* gradually take over their bodies and spirits, and they fall into a trance.

Macumba

Macumba is an African-Brazilian religion that is similar to Candomblé. It is practiced mainly in Rio de Janeiro, in the southeast. One main difference between Macumba and Candomblé is that *filhos* or *filhas de santo* who participate in Macumba ceremonies can be taken over by *orixás*, by forces of nature, or by the spirits of their **ancestors**, many of whom were slaves.

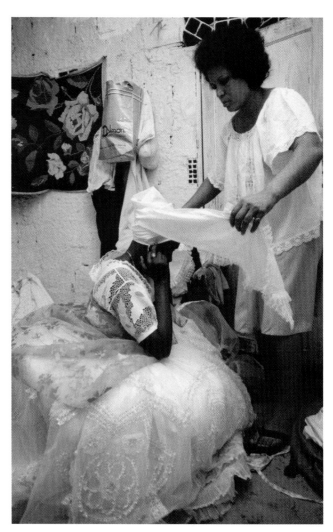

Two Macumba worshipers prepare for a candlelight ceremony in Rio de Janeiro.

Spirit protectors

Umbanda is practiced in Rio de Janeiro and São Paulo, also in the southeast. It is a combination of Candomblé, Macumba, and a religion called Kardecism, founded by a man from France named Alan Kardec. People who practice Umbanda believe that Catholic saints, *orixás*, and African and indigenous heroes can be their spirit protectors. To communicate with these spirits, priests and priestesses act like the spirit protectors. For example, if a priest is taken over by the spirit of an indigenous hunter, he might move his hands as if he is shooting a bow and arrow, like a hunter.

Other religions

Brazilians also practice other religions. People of Japanese ancestry, many of whom live in São Paulo, practice Shinto or Buddhism. Shinto began in Japan more than 1,000 years ago. Its followers worship their ancestors and spirits in nature. Buddhists believe they can escape life's sufferings by freeing themselves of all desires, leading truthful lives, resisting evil, not hurting others, and respecting all humans as equals.

Jewish people who **immigrated** mainly from Eastern Europe to Brazil believe in one God and follow teachings that are written in their holy book, the *Torah*. Many Brazilians from countries in the Middle East follow Islam. Followers of Islam, called Muslims, believe in one God, Allah, and obey his commands, which were revealed to the **prophet** Muhammad and are written in the *Qur'an*.

A Kaiowa shaman chants prayers in the southwestern state of Mato Grosso do Sul. The religious beliefs of Brazil's indigenous people are closely tied to the land and to the plants and animals that live there.

Christmas and the new year

Brazilian *festas*, or festivals, are times of great joy. Christmas, which is called *Natal* in Brazil, is on December 25. It celebrates the birth of Jesus Christ. Brazilians prepare for the holiday by setting up Nativity scenes, or *presépios*, in store windows, churches, and homes. The *presépios* show people and animals who were present at Jesus' birth. Fruits and models of animals from Brazil are also part of the scene.

Papai Noel, or Santa Claus, comes to visit early, dressed in a red and white suit with fur along the edges. Everyone else is in shorts! The seasons in Brazil are the opposite of seasons in North America, so Christmas falls in the summer. In Rio de Janeiro, Papai Noel arrives by helicopter at the Maracanã, the world's largest soccer stadium. Tens of thousands of excited children join him in singing Christmas carols, such as the Portuguese versions of "Silent Night" and "Away in a Manger," along with Brazilian carols, such as *"Repousa Tranquilo O Meigo Jesus,"* or "Lullaby for Baby Jesus." Then, Papai Noel gives the children small gifts.

The Christmas meal

Christmas dinner, called *ceia de Natal*, usually begins around midnight, after people return home from the Christmas church service, or Mass. *Ceia de Natal* often consists of ham or turkey with a special stuffing. To prepare the stuffing, Brazilians fry a coarse cornmeal-like grain made from the **manioc** plant in butter, then add turkey livers, onions, garlic, hard-boiled eggs, olives, raisins, and other dried fruit. *Rabanada* is a favorite dessert. It is made by soaking thick slices of bread in a mixture of beaten eggs and milk or wine, then frying the bread in oil and rolling it in cinnamon and sugar. After the Christmas meal, when everyone is asleep, Papai Noel sneaks in and leaves presents to be opened Christmas day.

A section of a Christmas mural in Salvador depicts familiar Christmas characters, such as Santa Claus and the Three Wise Men. It also shows famous Salvador landmarks, such as the Lighthouse of Barra and the Lacerda Elevator. The elevator takes people from the old part of the city, up above, to the new part, down below.

Fireworks light up the night sky over Rio de Janeiro's Copacabana Beach on New Year's Eve. Thousands of people pour onto the sand to greet the new year.

Folia de Reis

The *Folia de Reis*, or Festival of Kings, is held in Brazil's countryside. It honors the three wise men who brought gifts to the baby Jesus after he was born. During the festival, which is celebrated from December 24 to January 6, groups dressed in brightly colored costumes parade through the streets and into people's homes. They sing and perform dramatic dances, called *reisados*, that are based on Brazilian folktales. The main celebration takes place on the final night, January 6, which is called *Dia dos Reis*, or Kings' Day.

Awaken the new year

In Brazil, New Year's Eve is called *Réveillon*, which means "to awaken the new year." Dances, dinner parties, and fireworks mark the end of the old year and the beginning of the new. Brazilians have special *Réveillon* traditions to bring them luck. Some people believe that eating **lentils** at a midnight meal will bring wealth in the new year. People who hope for love in the new year wear a piece of red or pink clothing; those who wish for money wear yellow; and those praying for peace in their lives dress all in white. At midnight, Brazilians greet each other with kisses and with wishes of *"Feliz Ano Novo,"* or "Happy New Year."

During Carnaval, Salvador's streets are packed with crowds listening to the music of trio electricos, which are live bands that play on top of trucks.

Carnaval is the world's largest party. The rhythms of *samba* music fill the streets; *samba* dancers and musicians parade by in fancy costumes; and the smells of Brazilian foods waft through the air.

The origins of *Carnaval*

About 600 years ago, the Portuguese began to celebrate a festival called *Entrudo*. During *Entrudo*, people wore disguises and battled in the streets, throwing eggs, flour, soot, mud, dirty water, and bags filled with perfume. It was a last celebration before Lent, a 40-day period during which Catholics **fast** to remind themselves of the sufferings of Jesus Christ.

Early Portuguese settlers brought *Entrudo* to Brazil. Over time, people from other backgrounds added their customs to the holiday, which became known as *Carnaval*. In the late 1800s, African-Brazilians began to parade through the streets, dancing and beating African rhythms on their drums. This custom is still part of today's festivities, which take place in late February or early March.

Carnaval costumes, which include elaborate headdresses, take months to make.

Carnaval in Rio de Janeiro

Brazil's largest *Carnaval* is in Rio de Janeiro. For weeks before the holiday, groups of musicians and singers, called *blocos*, lead parades through the streets. *Carnaval* officially begins on the Friday before Lent, and ends five days later. Street parties break out all over. *Foliões*, who are people dressed in bathing suits or funny, homemade costumes, dance and act silly in the streets. Musicians play drums and brass instruments, inviting everyone to join in the fun.

Samba in the Sambódromo

The highlight of Rio's *Carnaval* are the *samba* parades. More than 80,000 members of *escolas de samba*, or *samba* schools, march through the grounds of the Sambódromo, a stadium built for *Carnaval*. The *escolas de samba* compete to see who has the best dancers, musicians, costumes, and floats.

Thousands of people fill the stands of the Sambódromo to watch the Carnaval parade.

Everybody *samba!*

Members of the *escolas de samba* prepare all year for the parade. First, they decide on a theme for their presentation, for example, a folktale or an historical event. Then, they compose *samba* music to go with the theme, practice dance steps, design costumes, and build elaborate floats. On the day of the parade, everything must be perfect to impress the judges and the 100,000 people who fill the Sambódromo. While the *bateria*, or **percussion** section, beats out the rhythm of the *samba*, the *passistas*, the school's best *samba* dancers, show off the steps they rehearsed all year. Hundreds of *Baianas*, who are women of African origin, twirl in big-hooped skirts, followed by huge, richly decorated floats called *carros alegóricos*.

Masquerade balls

In the 1840s, wealthy *cariocas*, as the people of Rio de Janeiro are called, wanted to celebrate *Carnaval* without going into the streets. They decided to hold masquerade balls, where they dressed in fancy costumes and wore masks so people would not recognize them.

Today, balls are an important part of *Carnaval* throughout Brazil. The most famous ball is the Copacabana Palace Ball, held in Rio. Politicians, actors, soccer players, and other celebrities attend this fancy ball, which has a different theme every year. The Hawaiian Ball is held around a swimming pool at the Rio Yacht Club and is known for its lavish decorations. At the Red and Black Ball, everyone wears red and black, the colors of Rio's soccer team. Tickets to balls are usually very expensive, so many people cannot afford to attend.

Carnaval in Recife

During *Carnaval* in the northeastern city of Recife, *frevo* dancers perform acrobatic moves such as twirling batons and small, colorful umbrellas from hand to hand and between their legs. They follow *frevo* bands marching through the streets or playing from platforms on the backs of trucks, called *freviocas*. The *maracatu* is one of Recife's *Carnaval* traditions. This **procession** acts out the crowning of an African "king" and "queen," whom the Portuguese chose to rule over African slaves. Some members of the "royal court" carry *calungas*, which are small dolls of African women dressed all in white. They believe that the *calungas* have magical powers that protect the people in the *maracatu*.

Olinda's puppet parade

The streets of Olinda, in northeastern Brazil, are so narrow that *Carnaval* floats, like those in Rio, cannot pass through. Instead, people parade with ten-foot (three-meter) puppets called *bonecos gigantes*. The puppets are usually characters from stories or people from the town's history. Each person who carries a puppet is almost completely covered by the puppet's skirt or pants. Only the person's eyes peek out through a small opening so he or she can see the way.

Carnaval celebrations in Recife begin with a large party called Galo da Madrugada. People wake up at dawn, dress in fancy costumes, and crowd onto downtown streets to sing and dance.

Puppet makers

Tharcio Botelho created the first *boneco gigante* in 1937. The puppet, which had a black top hat, tuxedo jacket with white buttons, and a gold tooth, was named O Homem da Meia-Noite, or the Midnight Man. A few years later, the puppet A Mulher do Dia, the Woman of the Day, was created to keep him company. The two were married at a ceremony attended by the people of Olinda. Soon, the puppets' family grew to include a daughter, A Menina da Tarde, or the Girl of the Afternoon, and a son, O Menino da Tarde, or the Boy of the Afternoon. The tradition of making gigantic puppets continues in Olinda today.

The giant puppets in Olinda's puppet parade are made of foam, papier mâché, and fiberglass. They are often dressed in jewelry and fancy clothes.

Honoring religious figures

Many Brazilian holidays honor **patron saints**. *Festa de Nossa Senhora de Aparecida*, or the Feast of Our Lady of the Appearance, honors the Virgin Mary, Brazil's patron saint. On the holiday, which takes place on October 12, people go on a pilgrimage to the southeastern town of Aparecida, where a special statue of the Virgin Mary stands. According to legend, in 1717, a fisher and two friends were having no luck catching fish. Desperate, the men prayed for help. The next time they pulled in their nets, there was a statue of the Virgin Mary. They flung their nets into the water one last time, pulled the nets out, and found thousands of fish. Today, many people visit the statue each year to ask the Virgin Mary to help them, just as she helped the fishers.

Gifts for the goddess of the sea

Many Brazilians who live along the coast worship Iemanjá, the African goddess of the sea. There are festivals to honor Iemanjá in different cities at different times of the year. In Rio de Janeiro, *Festa de Iemanjá*, or the Festival of Iemanjá, is celebrated on New Year's Eve. More than two million people, many dressed in white and carrying statues of the goddess, head to the beach to sing, dance, and watch fireworks. At midnight, they place makeup, mirrors, combs, hair ribbons, perfume, and other small gifts on rafts that they launch into the sea.

The procession of boats

Catholics throughout Brazil hold festivals at different times of the year to honor Nossa Senhora dos Navegantes, or Our Lady of Seafarers, and Nosso Senhor dos Navegantes, or Our Lord of Seafarers. Sailors and fishers believe that these patron saints watch over them. People in the southern city of Porto Alegre hold a procession of fishing boats on February 2 for *Festa de Nossa Senhora dos Navegantes*. Each boat carries a statue of Nossa Senhora dos Navegantes to a landing near a church. Then, people carry their statues to the church so that the priest can bless them.

Girls dressed in white carry a boat full of gifts for Iemanjá, the goddess of the sea. If the gifts sink, it is a sign that Iemanjá accepted their gifts and will grant their wishes. If the gifts float back to shore, their wishes have been refused.

Candomblé worshipers sweep the steps of the Igreja do Nosso Senhor do Bonfim at dawn. The church was built by a sea captain to thank God for saving him from drowning.

The washing of Bonfim

A festival called the *Lavagem do Bonfim*, or "the Washing of Bonfim," takes place in Salvador on the second Thursday of January. Early in the morning, Candomblé priestesses, dressed in white, wash the steps of the Igreja do Nosso Senhor do Bonfim, or the Church of Our Lord of Good End, until they are spotless. In the church square, people dance, eat, and buy Bonfim ribbons. The ribbons, which people wear around their wrists, each have three knots. The wearer makes one wish for each knot. When the ribbon falls off, the wishes are granted. There is one condition: someone must give you the ribbon for the wishes to come true. You cannot buy the ribbon yourself.

Festas Juninas

Three festivals in June, the *Festas Juninas*, honor saints Anthony, John, and Peter. Saint Anthony's Day, on June 12, honors the patron saint of lost possessions and of women looking for husbands. On this day, single women write the names of their boyfriends on small pieces of paper, fold them up, and place them in a bowl of water. If the paper unfolds, a woman will marry the man whose name she wrote.

Saint John spent his childhood in the countryside, so Saint John's Day, on June 24, celebrates country life. Everyone sings and dances around a large bonfire after eating baked sweet potatoes, *pé-de-moleque*, which is a kind of peanut brittle, and other country food. Saint Peter's Day, on June 28, honors the patron saint of fishers. To celebrate, a priest blesses people's decorated fishing boats and fish hooks.

People living in the Japanese community of Liberdade, in São Paulo, keep their traditions alive with fairs and cultural shows. A girl in colorful Japanese clothing and makeup participates in a parade.

Brazilian holidays mark important events in history and honor the traditions of Brazil's people. *Festa do 20 de Setembro*, or the Festival of September 20, is celebrated in the southern state of Rio Grande do Sul. It honors the *gaúchos*, or cowboys, who live in the area. During the festival, *gaúchos* parade through towns and cities on horseback. The parades are followed by balls and dances. *Festa do 20 de Setembro*, also known as *Festa Farroupilha*, is held on September 20 because it was on that day in 1835 that a group of *gaúchos*, led by Bento Gonçalves da Silva, began the Farroupilha Rebellion against Brazil's government. The *gaúchos* wanted Rio Grande do Sul to become a separate country. The rebellion lasted ten years before the government defeated the *gaúchos*.

Kayapó festivals

The Kayapó are an indigenous people who live in the Amazon rainforest, in the north. They hold festivals for entertainment, to mark life events, such as the naming of a child, and to celebrate the cycles of nature, for example, the beginning of the dry season or the harvest. During one holiday, the Corn Festival, dancers and singers painted with intricate designs and wearing colorful headdresses, beaded necklaces, and armbands retell the story of how corn was given to the Kayapó people.

Oktoberfest

For sixteen days in October, the people of Blumenau, in southern Brazil, celebrate the German festival of *Oktoberfest*. Many immigrants from Germany settled in the south during the 1800s. At *Oktoberfest*, people eat German sausages with sauerkraut, drink beer in the *biergarten*, or beer garden, and listen and dance to polka music. More than a million people attend the festival, drinking more than 200,000 gallons (909,200 liters) of beer each year.

The Pankararo, an indigenous people from the northeast, celebrate the harvest with a costumed dance called the tore.

17

The sounds and steps of Brazil

To play the berimbau, *an African instrument popular in Salvador, a musician holds a coin against a steel string and strikes it with a small stick. A gourd at the bottom of the instrument makes the sound stronger and deeper.*

If you listen carefully to Brazilian music, you will hear simple bamboo flutes called *pifes* and ten-foot- (three-meter-) long pipes called *uruas* which were first played by the country's indigenous people. *Cavaquinhos*, which are small guitars with four strings; *rabecas*, or fiddles; and accordions came from Portugal. People of African descent brought *tamborins*, which are small handheld drums that make high-pitched sounds when struck with sticks, and *berimbaus*, which look like wooden bows, with a steel string running from one end to the other.

In this presentation dance, men from the village of Kalapoló, in central Brazil, carry blowguns to show their skill as hunters.

Singing styles

Indigenous, African, and Portuguese people each brought their own style of singing to Brazil. Indigenous people often sing through their noses to make nasal sounds. Their songs have one-word choruses and verses that end on a low note. Africans contributed "call-and-response" songs. One singer calls out the verse and the other singers respond with the chorus. People from Portugal brought sentimental ballads, such as the *moda*, and a kind of lullaby called the *acalanto*.

Indigenous music and dance

Indigenous music and dance is often part of religious ceremonies. The Tukano people, who live in the Amazon rainforest, chant and dance in long lines with their arms over each other's shoulders. They take short, quick steps to the sounds of shakers made from small **gourds** filled with seeds. When groups of Yanomami, who also live in the Amazon rainforest, get together for a feast, the visiting group introduces itself with a presentation dance. The men rush up to their hosts, waving bows, arrows, sticks, and hatchets to show their strength. Girls follow, waving branches from palm trees, then boys arrive with small bows and arrows. Finally, the women dance in with their arms around each other's shoulders.

The *caboclinho*

The *caboclinho* is a traditional indigenous dance that depicts hunts, harvests, and battles. It is performed to the quick beat of pipes, drums, and rattles called *caracaxás*. Dancers wear short skirts, arm and leg bands, and elaborate headdresses — all decorated with long feathers — as they perform complicated steps. They lower themselves to the floor, spring back up again, and whirl around on their tiptoes and heels. *Caboclinho* dancers have to be in excellent shape to perform well.

From the northeast

Many of Brazil's music and dance styles come from the northeast and are based on styles that African slaves brought to the country. The *lundu* is a dance that a couple performs in the middle of a circle. One movement of the *lundu* is the *umbigada*, which means "belly button thrust," where dancers touch their belly buttons to one another. The *forró* is a quick-paced style of country dance and music played on accordions, drums, and triangles. *Música sertaneja* is Brazilian country and western music. Men dressed as cowboys sing about their lost loves and lonely lives.

The xaxado *is a folk dance from the northeast that is similar to a tap dance. The dance's name imitates the sound of hard boots scraping the dry ground of the region.*

A repentista *musician plays guitar in a park. Repentistas make up songs and lyrics as they sing.*

Born in Rio

In the 1870s, a new dance came out of Rio de Janeiro called the *maxixe*. It combined African rhythms, especially the *lundu*, with Cuban music and the European polka. Couples held their arms and heads steady, while moving their hips and feet, and wrapping their legs around each other. *Choro*, which means "to cry," also developed in the 1870s. *Choro* was the Brazilian version of European ballroom dances such as waltzes and polkas, with African music added. At first, *choro* musicians played only guitars, *cavaquinhos*, and flutes, but over time saxophones, clarinets, pianos, bass, and other percussion instruments were added. One of the most important *choro* performers was the flutist and saxophonist Pixinguinha (1897–1973). He was nicknamed "the Bach of *choro*."

Samba

The *samba*, Brazil's national music and dance, has its origins in the northeast but became popular in Rio de Janeiro. It combines many music and dance styles, especially the *lundu* and *maxixe*. Musicians play drums, tambourines, maracas, and other percussion instruments, as well as guitars, *cavaquinhos*, and brass instruments. Almost all Brazilians can dance the basic *samba*, but it takes years of practice to master the more difficult steps. For the basic *samba*, dancers keep their heads, arms, and shoulders very still while hopping lightly on one foot, brushing the other foot across the floor, and swinging their hips back and forth very quickly.

Samba styles and singers

Many types of *samba* are played throughout Brazil, in people's homes, on the streets, and in nightclubs. *Samba do morro*, or "**shantytown** samba," is played by large groups of musicians using only percussion instruments. *Samba enredo*, or "theme samba," is the *samba* of *Carnaval*, where one or two singers sing out the verse and thousands of people respond with the chorus.

Musicians invent new forms of *samba* all the time. The *samba pagode*, which began in the 1980s, is a return to the *samba* style in which small groups of musicians in bars and dance halls played simple rhythms. Singer Beth Carvalho (1946–) helped make *samba pagode* popular. Other famous samba singers include Martinho da Vila (1938–) and Bezerra da Silva (1937–). Da Vila is known for his work promoting African-Brazilian culture. Da Silva is known for singing about the difficulties of life in the *favelas*, or shantytowns, of large Brazilian cities instead of singing traditional *samba* songs about love.

Brazilian actress and singer Carmen Miranda helped popularize samba *music and dance in the 1950s. She appeared in several American movies and was famous for her tall headdresses piled with fruit.*

Bossa nova

Bossa nova is a combination of Brazilian *samba* and American jazz. It is often performed by one singer accompanied by a guitar, although sometimes a drum, saxophone, or piano is added. *Bossa nova* has a softer, quieter beat than *samba*, with more complicated rhythms. The popular Brazilian song "The Girl from Ipanema" made *bossa nova* a hit throughout the world.

Tropicalismo

Tropicalismo music was part of a movement in the late 1960s that also included new kinds of movies, theater, and poetry. *Tropicalismo* musicians combined traditional Brazilian musical styles and instruments with more modern sounds, such as rock n' roll. Songs often criticized the military, which took over the government in 1964. These songs were banned, and songwriters such as Caetano Veloso (1942–) and Gilberto Gil (1942–) were jailed or **exiled**.

Música popular brasileira

In the 1960s and 1970s, many new singers, songwriters, and musicians mixed Brazilian and international music styles so listeners could not tell whether they were hearing *samba* or jazz, *bossa nova* or reggae. They played a style of music known as *música popular brasileira*, or MPB. Chico Buarque (1944–) is one of the best known MPB singers and songwriters. His poetic lyrics, which often deal with political topics, have influenced other musicians.

Music today

Many *tropicalismo* and MPB musicians are still leading musical figures in Brazil. Gilberto Gil is considered the father of the Bahian sound, a combination of African rhythms and music from the Caribbean. There are also many new musical styles, such as Brazilian rap, rock, heavy metal, and techno music, that combine Brazilian music with styles from around the world.

Classical musicians rehearse for a performance at the Teatro Amazonas, an opera house in the northern city of Manaus.

Milton Nascimento (1942–) is an MPB singer whose songs tell of his love of Brazil's mountains, valleys, and rivers, and speak out against the unfair way in which the country's indigenous people are often treated.

Folk art

Brazilians' deep belief in the powers of saints and spirits to protect them from harm can be seen in their **folk art**. Craftspeople make images called ex-votos that Brazilians offer to saints as prayers or in thanks. Some ex-votos are in the shape of a body part that needs to be healed. Others are shaped like animals that are ill. Still others represent possessions that the owner wants to protect.

People who follow Candomblé wear good luck charms, such as *balangandãs*. A *balangandã* is a cluster of amulets, or charms, that ward off the "evil eye" and bring health and love. A *figa* also protects its owner from the "evil eye." A *figa* is a charm that is shaped like a clenched fist, with the thumb sticking out between the index finger and the middle finger. People say that a *figa* only works if it is received as a gift.

A father and daughter from the Juma tribe weave palm fronds to make baskets outside their home in the northwestern Amazon rainforest.

Carrancas

A hundred years ago, riverboat captains on the São Francisco River believed that evil spirits lurked in the water. To ward off these spirits, they put frightening carvings called *carrancas* on the fronts of their boats. The *carrancas* were half man, half beast, with wide-open mouths and sharp teeth. They were often painted in strong colors; shining white for the teeth, dark black for the eyes, and bright red for the lips and tongues. Today, most people do not believe in the powers of *carrancas*, although some fishers still place them on the fronts of their boats, and artists still make them as folk art.

Weaving

Weaving is a popular folk art in the Amazon and in the northeast. In the Amazon, indigenous people weave baskets and bags using grasses, leaves, and bark that they dye with plants and charcoal. They also weave simple hammocks, which they use as beds. **Artisans** in the northeast weave, embroider, or crochet more elaborate hammocks, with lace and cotton fringes.

A lacemaker in the northeastern city of Fortaleza spreads out her work on a large pillow so she can see the intricate design.

Lacemaking and carpet making

The northeastern states of Pernambuco and Bahia are famous for their lacemakers, called *rendeiras*. The *rendeiras* make very fine, detailed pieces of lace with geometric patterns or floral designs. It can take a lacemaker several months to make a tablecloth or a shawl, blouse, or skirt for a Candomblé ceremony.

In the area around Diamantina, a city in the southeast, artisans use a Portuguese type of needlework, called *arraiolo*, to make handmade rugs with complicated floral patterns and a tight weave. Artisans from this area also weave wall hangings, bedspreads, and other items with designs of flowers, dolls, houses, and churches.

Pottery

Potters in each region of Brazil use different types and colors of clay and decorate their work with different designs. In the Paraíba River Valley, in southeastern Brazil, potters make very detailed clay images of religious figures and of ordinary people living on farms and in villages.

On the northern island of Marajó, craftspeople make a type of pottery called *marajoara* using a technique that has been passed down for thousands of years. They take clay from the banks of the Amazon River; shape it into a pot, bowl, or water pitcher on a potter's wheel; dry it in the sun; and carve geometric patterns and animals into it. After they fire the piece, or harden it in a very hot oven, they paint and glaze it, which means that they cover it with a glossy finish that protects the paint.

Potters in Pernambuco use the region's reddish clay to make figures of the people in the area, including musicians in traditional costumes and farming families.

Painting and sculpture

Brazil's first artists were indigenous people who painted simple stick figures, geometric patterns, animals, and tools on cave walls. They also painted their bodies for special ceremonies, a tradition that continues today. The first Brazilians of Portuguese descent painted pictures of religious figures in the baroque style. Baroque art is dramatic and full of ornate details.

Aleijadinho created twelve soapstone sculptures of prophets from the Bible. The sculptures are displayed in front of a church in the southeastern town of Congonhas do Campo.

Aleijadinho

Antônio Francisco Lisboa (1738–1814) is Brazil's best known sculptor. He used Brazilian materials, such as soapstone and wood, to create figures and scenes from the Bible in the baroque style. Lisboa, who was nicknamed "Aleijadinho," which means "little cripple," created many of his best works after he developed a disease that crippled his hands. By tying a hammer and chisel to his wrists, he was still able to carve beautiful sculptures.

Brazil in art

After Brazil gained its independence from Portugal in 1822, artists began to paint realistic pictures of their country. José Ferraz de Almeida Júnior (1850–1899) was one of the first painters to put common people and everyday scenes in his work. Belmiro de Almeida (1858–1935) painted detailed scenes of wealthy Brazilians, showing their elaborate clothing and richly decorated mansions.

Modern art

In the 1920s, Brazilian artists began to paint people and places in less realistic ways. For example, Emiliano Di Cavalcanti (1897–1976) painted people, landscapes, and scenes from *Carnaval* in a cubist style. Cubist paintings look like they have been cut into small shapes and stuck together again. Another less realistic style of Brazilian painting is naïve art. Naïve artists, such as Heitor dos Prazeres (1898–1966), paint childlike scenes of everyday life in bright colors.

Rubem Valentim (1922–1991) is another modern Brazilian artist. His paintings and sculptures show images and objects from Candomblé. The Japanese-Brazilian painter Tomie Ohtake (1913–) paints **abstract** works with bright colors and simple curves and lines. Her paintings *Two Blue* and *Two Yellow* show paintbrush strokes of blue and yellow in the shape of an "x."

Cândido Portinari's painting Coffee Plantation, *created in 1935, shows farmhands working on a coffee plantation, picking and carrying heavy sacks of coffee beans. The workers' hands and feet are enlarged to show that work took up most of their lives.*

Cândido Portinari

Cândido Portinari (1903–1962) is considered one of Brazil's most important modern artists. The subjects of his paintings — slaves on plantations, farmers tilling fields, prospectors digging for gold, and wildlife in the rainforest — are often distorted to show their inner feelings and experiences. Portinari painted about 4,500 canvases before he died at the age of 59, poisoned by the lead in his oil paints.

Fabio Sombra is an artist from Rio de Janeiro who paints in the naïve style. He uses bright colors to show Brazilian scenes of red-tiled roofs, churches, and tropical plants.

Baroque and modern buildings

Brazilian cities are filled with beautiful churches, missions, and mansions. Most of these buildings were constructed in the 1600s and 1700s in the baroque style. They have many curved arches and are decorated with elaborate sculptures carved out of wood or stone. Indigenous craftspeople who worked on the buildings added their own touches, carving saints with indigenous-looking faces, bunches of tropical fruit, and palm trees.

Some of Brazil's cities — Brasília, the capital in the center of the country, Ouro Preto, in the southeast, and Olinda and Salvador, in the northeast — have so many impressive buildings that the United Nations Educational, Scientific, and Cultural Organization (UNESCO) has named them world heritage sites. World heritage sites are protected by UNESCO so that people from around the world can enjoy them.

Salvador

Salvador is known for its beautiful churches covered in gold. The interior of the Igreja de São Francisco, or Church of Saint Francis, is covered with carved angels, leaves, shells, and circular patterns, all painted in gold. The Igreja da Ordem Terceira de São Francisco, or Church of the Third Order of Saint Francis, has a stone front carved with many figures. The front was

plastered over for 150 years until a worker repairing the church discovered the carvings underneath. Since then, the carvings have been restored. The Catedral Basílica, or Cathedral of Bahia, has walls covered in marble and a ceiling covered in *azulejos*, which are ceramic tiles; frescoes, which are pictures painted on plaster; and wooden carvings painted in gold.

(top) Early Portuguese explorers built elaborate homes in the town of Olinda, a name meaning "how beautiful" in Portuguese. Today, many artists and musicians live in these restored historic houses.

(left) Carved scrolls, ribbons, and people cover the exterior of this building in Olinda.

Olinda

Olinda is filled with baroque churches, palaces, and homes. In the early 1600s, it was the center of the country's sugar industry, but Dutch invaders destroyed most of its buildings in 1631. The buildings have been reconstructed. The Convento de São Francisco, or Convent of Saint Francis, is considered by many to be Olinda's most beautiful building. It consists of a **convent**, chapel, and church. On the walls of the church, *azulejos* panels tell the story of the Virgin Mary, while the **cloister** features *azulejos* with scenes from the life of Saint Francis of Assisi.

Ouro Preto

Ouro Preto, meaning "black gold," was the center of the gold rush in the 1700s. The city was named for the black gold, which was really gold mixed with iron ore, found in nearby streams. Among its many impressive baroque buildings is the Igreja de Nossa Senhora do Carmo, the Church of Our Lady of Carmo. The church was designed by Aleijadinho's father, the **architect** Manual Francisco Lisboa, and completed by Aleijadinho after his father's death. Bell towers stand at each end of the church, and an elegant archway decorated with stone carvings rises above the main door. Inside the church, Aleijadinho's carvings of figures painted in gold seem to jump out of the many **altars**. The ceiling is painted with scenes from the Bible that are enclosed in elaborate gold frames.

A beautiful old-style church in Olinda shows the architectural style of colonial buildings of the 1700s.

Brasília

Brasília was built between 1957 and 1960 to encourage people to move to the country's interior. The city was planned by Lúcio Costa and designed by architect Oscar Niemeyer and **landscape architect** Burle Marx. Most of Niemeyer's buildings have very simple designs, and are made with concrete and glass. The Palácio do Itamarati, or Itamarati Palace, is home to the Ministry of Foreign Affairs. The building, which sits in a pool of water, looks like a square of glass surrounded by a concrete roof and huge concrete arches. The Catedral Metropolitana, or National Cathedral, is built in the shape of an upside down **chalice** and a crown of thorns, which Jesus wore.

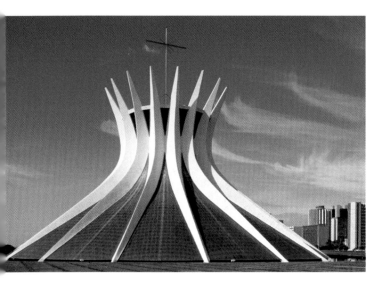

Most of Brasília's Catedral Metropolitana, which has a stained glass ceiling from which aluminum sculptures hang, is underground.

A man relaxes in a park with a good book in the southern city of Porto Alegre.

Brazil's official language is Portuguese, but it is not the same as the Portuguese spoken in Portugal. Brazilian Portuguese has its own vocabulary, including tens of thousands of words from indigenous and African languages. For example, the words for pineapple, *abacaxi*; cashew, *caju*; and armadillo, *tatu*, all come from Tupi, an indigenous language. Words from Quimbundo and other African languages include *caçula*, meaning the youngest child, *moleque*, meaning young boy, and *vatapá*, a creamy seafood or chicken stew. Brazilian Portuguese also has its own accents, especially in the central and southern parts of the country where many European immigrants settled, and in the northeast, where people of African origin settled.

Languages of indigenous peoples

Brazil's indigenous peoples speak 180 languages, most of which can be divided into four main groups: Macro-Tupi, Macro-Jê, Karib, and Aruak. Before the Portuguese arrived, these languages were only spoken, not written, but in the past 500 years many languages have been given written symbols and a grammar.

The first indigenous people that the Portuguese met spoke Tupi, one of the Macro-Tupi languages. Jesuit missionaries studied and taught Tupi, and it is still the language best known to non-indigenous people. Many indigenous languages are disappearing as indigenous people come in contact with people of Portuguese descent. Today, many children are learning their native language in addition to Portuguese.

English	Portuguese
Hello.	*Alô* or *olá*.
Goodbye.	*Tchau* or *até logo*.
Pleased to meet you.	*Muito prazer*.
What is your name?	*Qual é o seu nome?*
My name is…	*Meu nome é…*
Please.	*Faça favor* or *por favor*.
Thank you.	*Obrigado* (males), *obrigada* (females).
Yes.	*Bem* or *sim*.
No.	*Não*.

In Aguacu on the Argentinian border, a man waits at a bus stop or onibus, *while he reads a Portuguese-language newspaper.*

Brazil's early writers

The first Brazilian writers of the 1500s wrote mostly letters and stories about life in the new **colony**. One of the best known writers of the 1600s was Gregório de Matos Guerra (1636–1696), who wrote religious and satirical poetry. In his verses, de Matos Guerra made fun of people he did not agree with. Long epic poems in the 1700s often described life in the country in a simple, romantic way. Other poems told of love. Tomás Antonio Gonzaga (1744–1810) wrote beautiful five-line poems, called *liras*, in honor of the woman he loved.

Brazilian realism

In the 1800s, writers began to produce realistic novels and poems about the struggles of Brazilian life. Aluísio Azevedo (1857–1913) wrote *O Cortiço*, or *A Brazilian Tenement*, which describes the difficult lives of working-class Brazilians in cities. Euclides da Cunha's (1866–1901) novel *Os Sertões*, or *Rebellion in the Backlands*, tells about army attacks on religious **rebels** in the northeast. Joaquim Maria Machado de Assis (1839–1908) is considered Brazil's greatest novelist. His book *Memorias Posthumas de Braz Cubas*, or *Epitaph of a Small Winner*, starts with the narrator's death, then goes back in time as the narrator describes his life in 160 short chapters.

Brazilian author Paulo Coelho lies in a pile of his novels, which have been translated from Portuguese into 55 languages.

Modern writers

Mário de Andrade (1893–1945) was a poet and novelist who traveled in Brazil's interior and wrote about the indigenous people. His novel *Macunaíma* tells of an indigenous man who leaves the Amazon to live in São Paulo. Graciliano Ramos (1892–1953) was born in the *sertão*, or backlands, of northeastern Brazil. In his novel *Vidas Secas*, or *Barren Lives*, the family of a cattle herder leaves a difficult life in the **drought**-ridden *sertão*, but finds that surviving in the big city can be just as challenging.

Clarice Lispector (1920–1977) became one of the best female writers in **Latin America**. Among her novels, which are usually about the lives of women, is *A Hora de Estrela*, or *The Hour of the Star*. It tells the story of Macabéa, a typist living in poverty in Rio de Janeiro. Jorge Amado (1912–2001) told colorful stories of common people struggling to survive in northeastern Brazil. In his novel *Dona Flor e Seus Dois Maridos*, or *Dona Flor and Her Two Husbands*, Dona Flor remarries after her first husband dies. Despite death, he keeps reappearing.

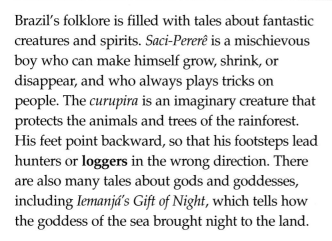

A Brazilian myth

Brazil's folklore is filled with tales about fantastic creatures and spirits. *Saci-Pererê* is a mischievous boy who can make himself grow, shrink, or disappear, and who always plays tricks on people. The *curupira* is an imaginary creature that protects the animals and trees of the rainforest. His feet point backward, so that his footsteps lead hunters or **loggers** in the wrong direction. There are also many tales about gods and goddesses, including *Iemanjá's Gift of Night*, which tells how the goddess of the sea brought night to the land.

Iemanjá's Gift of Night

Many, many years ago, when the world was new, there was no night. The earth was filled with day, sunlight, and heat all the time. The great African goddess Iemanjá lived in the dark depths of the sea. One day, Iemanjá's daughter fell in love with a son of the earth and went to live with him in the land of daylight.

At first, Iemanjá's daughter was happy to live on land. Her husband was kind and gentle. He showed her the wonders of earth — the bright, sandy beaches, the rows of cocoa trees and sugar cane, and the colorful costumes worn at festivals. Over time, though, the bright sunlight began to burn her eyes.

"Oh, how I long for the night," Iemanjá's daughter cried to her husband. "What is night?" he asked, concerned for his wife's great sorrow. "It is the cool shadows and dark corners," she replied. "If only we could bring a small part of my mother's kingdom here, so that we would have darkness at times to rest our weary eyes."

Her husband called for his three most trusted servants. He told them to go to Iemanjá and beg her for a small piece of darkness for her daughter, whose sorrow grew each day.

The servants embarked on a long, dangerous journey through rough waves, sharp coral reefs, and shifting underwater sands. When they arrived at Iemanjá's palace, they begged her for a piece of night.

Without wasting a moment, Iemanjá packed a bag for the servants to take to her beloved daughter. Then, she spoke to them sternly, "Do not open this bag until you reach my daughter, for she is the only one who can calm the night spirits inside."

As the servants headed home through the waves and along the shore, the creatures inside the bag began to make strange sounds, screeches, and screams. The first servant trembled uncontrollably. The second wanted to drop the bag and run. The third opened the bag to see what was inside.

Night beasts, night birds, and night insects rushed out of the bag, followed by the moon and stars. Iemanjá's daughter saw what happened, and called out to the spirits, "I am the daughter of the goddess Iemanjá and I greet you, spirits of the night." As she spoke, the night spirits became calm and quiet darkness covered the land.

The darkness soothed Iemanjá's daughter's eyes and she soon fell into a deep sleep. When she awoke, she felt more refreshed than she had since coming to live on the land. Finally, she felt at home in her husband's world. To celebrate her happiness, she gave three gifts to the land. Her gifts — the bright morning star, the rooster's warning voice, and the birds' beautiful songs — still announce the beginning of each new day.

Glossary

abstract Describing art that represents objects using shapes, lines, and color

altar A table or stand used for religious ceremonies

ancestor A person from whom one is descended

architect A designer of buildings

artisan A skilled craftsperson

chalice A large decorative cup used in religious ceremonies

cloister A covered passage around an open square in a church or monastery

colony An area controlled by a distant country

convent A home for nuns, or women devoted to the Catholic Church

convert To change one's religion, faith, or beliefs

denomination An organized religious group within a faith

descent Ethnic background

drought A long period of time when no rain falls

exiled Forced from one's native country

fast To stop eating food or certain kinds of food for religious or health reasons

fertility The ability to produce children

folk art Art reflecting the traditional culture of a people or country

gourd The hard-shelled fruit of certain vines

immigrate To settle in another country

indigenous Native to a country

landscape architect A person who designs gardens

Latin America The Spanish-, French-, and Portuguese-speaking countries south of the United States

lentil A round seed that can be eaten

logger A person who cuts down forests

manioc A starchy root vegetable

missionary A person who travels to a foreign country to spread a particular religion

patron saint A saint who is believed to protect a person, profession, city, or country

percussion Relating to musical instruments played by hitting, shaking, or scraping

pilgrimage A journey to a special religious place

plantation A large farm on which crops such as cotton and sugar are grown

preacher A person who gives religious speeches

procession A group of persons or vehicles moving along in an orderly, formal manner

prophet A person who is believed to speak on behalf of God

rebel A person who opposes a government or ruler

resistance The body's natural ability to fight off disease

sacrifice To kill in a religious ceremony as an offering to gods

shantytown A poor area of a city with many makeshift houses

Index

Africans 4, 5, 8–9, 12, 13, 14, 15, 18, 19, 21, 28, 30–31
Aleijadinho 24, 27
architecture 5, 6, 26–27
art 22–25
Batista, Father Cícero Romão 6–7
Brasília 26, 27
Bumba-meu-boi 4
Candomblé 8, 16, 22
Carnaval 5, 12–14, 20
Christianity 5, 6–8, 9–10, 12, 15–16, 22

Christmas 10–11
dance 12–13, 14, 17, 18–20
festivals 4, 10–17
folklore 30–31
food 10, 11, 16, 28
gaúchos 17
Iemanjá 8, 15, 30–31
indigenous peoples 4, 5, 6, 8, 9, 17, 18–19, 21, 22, 24, 26, 28
immigrants 9, 17, 28
language 5, 28
Macumba 8

music 4, 5, 12, 13, 14, 17, 18–21
New Year 11, 15
Oktoberfest 17
Olinda 14, 26, 27
Ouro Preto 26, 27
poetry 20, 29
Portinari, Cândido 25
Porto Alegre 15
Portuguese 4, 5, 6, 12, 14, 18, 23, 24, 26, 28
puppets 14
Recife 14
religion 5, 6–11, 12,

15–16, 18, 22
Rio de Janeiro 5, 8, 10, 11, 12–13, 15, 19, 20
Roman Catholicism 5, 6–7, 8, 12, 15, 16, 22
saints 6, 9, 15, 16, 22
Salvador 5, 6, 8, 10, 12, 16, 26
samba 12–13, 20
São Paulo 9, 17
Umbanda 9
writers 29

1 2 3 4 5 6 7 8 9 0   Printed in the USA   0 9 8 7 6 5 4 3